Instant Etiquette
for
Businessmen

Instant Etiquette

for

Businessmen

by

Lileth MacKnight

ILLUSTRATIONS BY M. E. PALM

Published by ARC Books, Inc.,
219 Park Avenue South, New York, N.Y. 10003
Copyright © by ARC BOOKS, INC., 1966
*All rights reserved. No part of this book may be reproduced,
by any means, without permission in writing from the
publishers.*
Library of Congress Catalog Card Number: 66-20383
Printed in the United States of America

ACKNOWLEDGMENTS

My thanks to the many friends and strangers (seat-mates on planes, in club cars, buses and limousines; met in restaurants and bookstores), all men, for sharing their pet peeves and opinions on etiquette; for their advice; for completing my questionnaire on tipping; and, most of all, for taking me seriously!

Special thanks to:

Lawrence Pucci

Frank J. Gillespie, Jr., Conrad Hilton Hotel, Chicago

A group of cadets from Missouri Military Academy, who, by their trim appearance, excellent table manners and unmonitored good behavior in the St. Louis airport, unwittingly provided the inspiration for *Instant Etiquette for Businessmen*

CONTENTS

CONTENTS

Chapter 1

INTRODUCTIONS

wrong

MAN to MAN

When you introduce one man to another, *don't say:*

"Mr. Bell, meet Mr. Jordan."

"Mr. Bell, shake hands with Mr. Jordan."

"Mr. Bell, I want to make you acquainted with Mr. Jordan," etc.

MAN to WOMAN

When you introduce a man to a woman (socially) *don't* give *his* name *first:*

"Mr. Bell, meet Miss Barnes."

"Mr. Bell, I want to make you acquainted with Miss Barnes."

INTER-OFFICE: *The Boss*

When you introduce an employee (man or woman) to superior, *don't* give *superior's* name *last:*

"Miss Secretary, this is Mr. Vice President."

"Mr. Bookkeeper, this is Mr. Vice President."

"Miss Clerk, Mr. Sales Manager."

NEW EMPLOYEE

Don't use first names only:

"Jack, this is Dave."

"Ann, this is Mary."

right

MAN to MAN

Say:

"Mr. Bell, Mr. Jordan."

"Mr. Bell, this is Mr. Jordan."

"Mr. Bell, this is my assistant, Mr. Jordan (or Bob Jordan)."

If you are walking with Jordan and meet your friend Bell, after greeting Bell, you might say:

"Jack, this is Bob Jordan . . . Jack Bell."

MAN to WOMAN (Socially)

Give *her* name *first:*

"Miss Barnes, Mr. Bell" (or "Ann Barnes, Jack Bell").

"Miss Barnes, this is Mr. Bell."

INTER-OFFICE: *The Boss*

To introduce a man or woman employee to a *business* superior give *superior's* name *first:*

"Mr. Vice President, my secretary Miss Barnes (or Ann Barnes)."

"Mr. Vice President, Mr. Bookkeeper."

"Mr. Sales Manager, Miss Clerk."

NEW EMPLOYEE

To introduce a new employee to co-workers, *say:*

"This is Mr. Bell (or John Bell), who will be on our production staff . . . Mr. Mayer (or Dave Mayer) our director of marketing," or "Jack Bell, Dave Mayer."

"This is Mary Allen, who is new in our filing department . . . Miss Barnes (or Ann Barnes), my secretary," or "Ann Barnes, Mary Allen."

Note: Some businesses stress the use of first names. You may be on a first-name basis with the Boss, but you *never* call him by his first name if an outsider is present.

wrong

To acknowledge an introduction (man or woman) *don't say:*

"Pleased to meet you." ("Pleased to meetcha" is worse!)

"Pleased to make your acquaintance."

"My pleasure," "Pleased, I'm sure," etc.

Never remain seated when introduced.*

* See exception page 11.

right

Acknowledge an introduction by saying:
"How do you do?"
"How do you do, Mr. Bell?"
When introduced to a group, you might say, "How do you do, Mr. Bell . . '." then repeat each man's name as you shake his hand, "Mr. Jordan . . . Mr. Hill . . . Mr. Mayer . . . etc."

ON YOUR FEET!
Always stand when introduced.*

If introduced to a woman after everyone is seated at dining table, hold onto napkin, rise briefly an inch or two from chair (more a motion than actually rising), say, "How do you do?" If caught with your mouth full, just nod.

If you are dining with a woman, stand immediately if anyone (man or woman) stops at your table. Remain standing until he or she leaves.

* *Exception:* After everyone is seated at conference table, it is customary just to nod and repeat the man's name.

wrong

YOURSELF

To introduce yourself, *don't say:*
"I'm *Mister* Hill."

YOUR WIFE

~~To~~ introduce your wife, *don't say:*
"Mr. Jordan, this is my wife, *Mrs.* Hill."
"Mr. Jordan, this is Marian."
"Meet my better half," "the missus," etc.

SHAKE HANDS

Don't fail to shake hands with a man, *but—*
Don't shake hands with a woman unless she offers her hand *first.*
Don't pump hand up and down.
Don't make handshake a bonecrusher or as limp as a dead fish.

right

YOURSELF

    To introduce yourself, *say:*

        "I'm George Hill."

YOUR WIFE

    To introduce *anyone** to your wife, give *her* name *first;* call her *your wife:*

        "Marian, this is Mr. Jordan . . . my wife."

SHAKE HANDS

    Always shake hands with a man when introduced. With a woman *only* if she offers *her* hand *first.* Make handshake *brief* but *firm.*

---

*Exception: To introduce your wife to a much older woman, a distinguished guest (man or woman), *say:* "Mrs. Vice President, this is my wife Marian," or "I'm George Hill, Mr. Speaker, and this is my wife."

13

wrong

Don't keep your hat on: when introduced to a woman.

Or when you meet a woman on the street, lobby, hall or elsewhere and stop to talk.

Don't tip your hat to another man.

right

TAKE OFF YOUR HAT

When you are introduced to a woman or stop to talk briefly. If you decide to walk along with her, put on your hat.

TIP YOUR HAT (briefly touch the brim)

To a woman whenever hello, goodby, thank you, you're welcome, excuse me, etc., are spoken or implied.

When walking with a woman and she greets someone, man *or* woman.

15

Chapter 2

THE TELEPHONE

wrong

ANSWERING THE PHONE

Don't say "hello" when answering a business phone *unless all your calls are screened* by switchboard operator or secretary.

If you *do* answer an unscreened call by saying "hello" and the caller asks for you, *don't* say: "This is *Mr.* Hill," or "This is he," or "Talking."

EXTENSIONS

If you share an extension, *don't* say "hello" and *don't* say "accounting" or "advertising department" without giving your name.

WRONG NUMBER

If you reach a wrong number, *don't* say:

"What number *is* this?" (This brings on "What number are you calling?" and gets you nowhere.)

Never just hang up with a crash *without saying anything*.

If a call is directed to you in error, *don't* hang up until you have signaled switchboard, and explained the mistake.

right

ANSWERING THE PHONE

To answer a business phone, *say:*

"Universal Products, George Hill."

or

"Universal Products, Hill."

To answer your own extension, *say:*

"George Hill," or "Hill."

If you prefer "hello," say it only when *all* your calls are screened and there is no doubt that it is *you.*

If you *do* answer an unscreened call by saying "hello" and caller asks for you, say: "This is George Hill."

EXTENSIONS

If you share an extension, answer by *saying:*

"Accounting Department, Hill" (or "George Hill").

or

"Extension 402, Hill."

If you answer another man's phone, *say:*

"Mr. Bell's office" or "Mr. Bell's desk."

WRONG NUMBER

If you reach a wrong number, *say:*

"Is this 722-0500?" (the number you dialed)

The answer to that is: "No, you have the wrong number."

You then say, "I'm sorry" and hang up *quietly.*

If a call is directed to you in error, *be helpful. Stay on the line* until switchboard has been informed and taken the call.

wrong

MAKING A CALL

When you make a business call, *don't* say to the person who answers:

"*Hello*, may I speak to Mr. Smith?"

"Hello, Mr. Smith, please."

"Is Mr. Smith in?"

"I wanna talk to Mr. Smith."

"Lemme talk to Bill Smith."

"Bill Smith there?"

"What's the guy's name who handles your printing?"

Do not fail to identify yourself immediately to call-screener.

She should not have to ask: "Who's calling, please?"

THE BOSS ANSWERS

If you are connected with Mr. Smith direct and you recognize his voice when he says "hello," unless you are a personal friend, *don't* say:

"Is this Mr. Smith?"

or

"Mr. Smith?"

GOOD-BY

Don't hang up abruptly without some indication that conversation is ended and don't add any frills such as "Good-by, now."

right

MAKING A CALL

To the switchboard operator of a large company, *say:*

"Mr. Smith, please."

Identify yourself immediately to the person who answers next:

"This is George Hill of Universal Products.

May I speak to Mr. Smith, please?"

or (if you call Smith frequently):

"This is George Hill. May I speak to Mr. Smith, please?"

To the receptionist-switchboard (or call-director) operator of a smaller office:

Identify yourself immediately and ask for Mr. Smith.

In either case, be ready to identify yourself to the operator if she hesitates to ring Smith. If you are not sure Smith knows who you are, repeat your name when *he* answers.

THE BOSS ANSWERS

If his secretary is out, Mr. Smith may answer his own phone by saying: "hello" (his calls are usually screened). Identify yourself in the usual way, even though you recognize his voice:

"This is George Hill. May I speak to Mr. Smith?"

He then says: "This is Bill Smith" or "This is Smith."

GOOD-BY

End calls with "good-by" or *omit it* when *both* parties *know* conversation is ended.

wrong

MISCELLANEOUS

Don't talk to someone on the phone and someone at your desk at the same time.

Don't call yourself *Mister* except when calling a woman on business:

"Mrs. Hall? This is Joe Hardy of Brown's."

Don't forget that a good telephone voice is important. *Don't* mumble, shout, be timid or gruff.

right

Talk to one person at a time. If someone interrupts while you are on the phone, say, "Excuse me a minute, please," cover mouthpiece, answer question—say, "I'm sorry," when you resume conversation.

Call yourself *Mister* when calling a woman on business: "Mrs. Bell? This is *Mr.* Hardy of Brown's."

Cultivate a good telephone voice. Make yours *distinct, friendly, attentive.*

wrong

When you ask your secretary or switchboard operator to get someone on the phone for you:

> *Don't leave your office or fail to be on the line when he answers!*

If you, Gordon, ask your secretary to get Mr. Murray, *Don't* let this happen:

Gordon's secretary to Murray's secretary:

"Mr. Gordon of Gordon Engineering calling Mr. Murray."

Murray's secretary to Murray:

"Mr. Gordon, Gordon Engineering, calling you."

Murray to his secretary:

"Is he on the line?"

Murray's secretary to Gordon's secretary:

"Put Mr. Gordon on, please."

Gordon's secretary to Murray's secretary:

"Is Mr. Murray on the wire?" etc., etc., etc.

right

You, Gordon, ask your secretary to get Mr. Murray:
Be on the line when he answers!

Gordon's secretary to Murray's secretary:

"Mr. Gordon of Gordon Engineering calling Mr. Murray."

Murray's secretary to Murray:

"Mr. Gordon, Gordon Engineering, calling you."

Murray's secretary to Gordon's secretary:

"Here's Mr. Murray."

Murray picks up the phone and says:

"Hello, Mr. Gordon," or "Hello, Paul."

Gordon's secretary has signalled him, he is on the line and says:

"Hello, Mr. Murray," or "Hello, Ed," etc.

Chapter 3

THE OFFICIAL CALL

wrong

KEEPING AN APPOINTMENT

Don't be late. That means you start with an apology.
Don't have brief case in disorder, rumpled samples, etc.

right

KEEPING AN APPOINTMENT
Be on time. A few minutes early is better!
Have brief case and samples in good order.

wrong

Don't keep hat on while talking to receptionist—and no extra conversation or wise cracks.

Don't pace the floor, tap on table, chew gum, whistle, or smoke unless ash trays are provided.

Don't toss coat in a pile or remain seated if secretary or Mr. Jordan appears.

right

Take off your hat as you approach receptionist, identify yourself, tell her whom you want to see. Thank her, follow her instructions. (She often gets you in or keeps you out!)

Smoking optional—*if ash tray is available*.

Keep your hat off, remove overcoat, hang on rack or fold and place on lap or chair. *Stand* if secretary or Mr. Jordan appears.

wrong

KEEPING AN APPOINTMENT

Don't hesitate to repeat your name and *don't* offer to shake hands unless Jordan offers first.

Don't sit until invited to do so or smoke unless Jordan suggests it.

Don't stay too long and *don't* forget to thank receptionist on your way out.

RECEIVING A CALLER

Don't keep caller waiting if he has an appointment. If you agree to see him, without an appointment, *don't* feel free to keep him waiting indefinitely.

Don't remain seated when he enters your office or forget that he expects *you* to *offer* to shake hands *first*.

Don't admit him to your office, then let him stand or sit while you talk at length on the phone, carry on an obviously trivial conversation with your secretary or a co-worker, doodle absent-mindedly, shuffle through papers on your desk.

Don't be rude if he overstays and *Don't* forget to stand when he leaves.

right

KEEPING AN APPOINTMENT

Say, "I'm George Hill," if Jordan does not greet you by name, and wait for him to offer to shake hands.

Stand until he tells you to sit and smoke only if he suggests it.

Be alert to signs that he wishes to end interview.

Thank receptionist on your way out.

RECEIVING A CALLER

If caller has an appointment, see him as promptly as possible. If delay is unavoidable, have receptionist or secretary so advise him. Say, "I'm sorry to have kept you waiting," when you do see him.

Stand when he enters your office.

It is customary to shake hands. *You offer your hand* first.

Ask him to be seated and give him your complete attention.

End interview courteously if he stays too long. ("I'm sorry but I have to attend a meeting in a few minutes.")

Stand when he leaves.

Shaking hands at parting is optional but customary.

Chapter 4

SMOKING

wrong

DON'T IGNORE A NO SMOKING SIGN

Don't smoke in elevators or outside your own office, section or department unless you know it's acceptable.

Don't put burning cigaret on edge of desk, windowsill, file cabinet, watercooler, etc.

right

A *No Smoking* sign means *No Smoking. Obey It!*

SMOKE: In your own office.
At your own desk.
In someone else's office by invitation.
Elsewhere in offices or building if you're sure it's acceptable.

Use ash tray for burning cigaret.

wrong

Don't let cigaret burn out. *Never* rub out on floor or dip in coffee or water in drinking glass.

Don't let ashes fall anywhere but in ash tray—not in plate or saucer at dining table, not on someone else's desk and *especially not on you!*

right

Be neat—keep ash tray reasonably clean, *especially* if you smoke cigars.

Smoke your *pipe* at your own desk.

Put cigaret *out* (in ash tray) when leaving desk or when you are through smoking.

wrong

Don't let smoke blow in anyone's face.

Don't let nicotine stain teeth or fingers.

Don't forget to offer others a cigaret when smoking (a constant borrower *not* included) and *don't be* a constant borrower!

Don't talk or shake hands with cigar, cigaret (one eye squinting) or pipe in mouth.

right

Keep smoke out of your neighbor's face.

Keep teeth and fingers free from nicotine stains.
In a group, other than co-workers, offer cigarets to men or women, before taking one yourself.

Buy your own!

Chapter 5

THE BUSINESS LUNCH

wrong

THE HOST

THE INVITATION
When you invite a man to lunch, for business reasons, *don't say*: "Let's have lunch together." (This suggests that each pay his own.)

THE DATE
Don't say: "*I* can make it Wednesday or Thursday." (Gives the idea you're available only on those days.)

THE PLACE
Don't ask him where he'd like to eat without *naming* a restaurant or two or a club.

THE TIME
Do not say: "I can make it at 12:30" or "One's a good time for me—how about you?" etc.

Don't take him to a restaurant where you'll have to stand in line for any length of time.

Don't be late and *never* go to table without him, unless you have more than one guest. (A prompt guest should not have to stand and wait for a very tardy one.)

right

THE HOST

YOU INVITE HIM
Say: "How about having lunch with me?"
or
"Could you have lunch *with me* next week?"

THE DATE
Be definite. *Say:* "Next Tuesday or Wednesday?"
He chooses.

THE PLACE
Suggest one or two places, if possible. If he says either one, *you* decide.

THE TIME
Suggest a time, 12:30 or 1:00, between 12:00 and 1:00, etc.
He decides.
Make a reservation, if necessary.

Be there a little early, check your hat, wait in anteroom. If one guest out of a group is more than ten minutes late, go to table but leave your name and guest's name with head waiter.

wrong

COCKTAILS?

Don't say: "Do you want a drink?" *don't* insist if he says no—and *don't* have one yourself if there are no other guests who are drinking at the table.

Never insist on a second round, nor order seconds without giving guest a chance to refuse.

Don't talk business before ordering unless guest brings it up first.

right

COCKTAILS?

Say: "How about a cocktail" or "What would you like to drink?"

Order no drink for yourself if he says no, but you should join any guest at your table who has a drink. If you don't drink at all, join a guest who is by ordering tomato juice or a similar non-alcoholic beverage.

wrong

THE FOOD

Don't say: "Why don't you have roast beef?" "Let's have a steak," etc. Never order for him.

He's your guest—but *don't* fuss over him!

right

THE FOOD

You might suggest: "Seafood is good here," or "Roast beef is the specialty," etc.

He chooses and gives his own order to waiter.

Be casual about seeing that he is comfortable, has what he wants and needs—ash tray, more coffee, anything waiter overlooks.*

Now you talk business.

* If your guest is a woman, the same rules apply, except that (if waiter does not) you pull out her chair and give it a slight push as she seats herself. She gives her order to you or to waiter direct.

wrong

THE CHECK

Don't interrupt conversation to study amount, audibly check or comment on it, or refer to expense account.

Never permit guest to pay all or any part of check.

Don't leave tip in nickels and dimes—*never* include pennies.

right

THE CHECK

   Glance at it casually and as briefly as possible.

Have money or credit card handy.

Leave tip in quarters and up, or add to credit card.

wrong

THE GUEST

THE DATE—*Don't* play "hard to get."

THE TIME—*Don't* choose the hour and then be late.

COCKTAIL?—*Don't say:* "I'll have one if you do," or "Never drink at lunch."

THE FOOD—*Don't* study menu from cover to cover; ask for substitutions, make ordering difficult.

THE CHECK—*Never* look at check, comment on it, or offer to pay any part of it.

DEPARTURE—*Don't* stay too long after eating.

right

THE GUEST

THE DATE—After you accept, choose a day host suggests, if possible.

THE TIME—Be specific as to time, arrive promptly.

COCKTAIL?—Feel free to order or refuse cocktail. *Say:* "I'll have a martini" or "No, thanks."

THE FOOD—Order as quickly as possible.

THE CHECK—Ignore it!

DEPARTURE—*It's your move.* Be alert, watch for signs host has to get back to office, make the first move to leave.

ARE YOU OBLIGATED?—No return luncheon necessary or expected.

Chapter 6

OFFICIAL PARTIES, DINNERS, AND BANQUETS

OFFICIAL PARTIES

Printed or engraved invitations to *large* official luncheons, cocktail parties or banquets are addressed to business addresses, require acceptances or regrets (made by cards enclosed for that purpose, by telephone or telegram, or by letter on business stationery).

No wives, relatives or friends attend unless *specifically included*.

DINNER GUESTS

If you take a man to dinner, the same rules apply as at lunch.

If he is from out-of-town and his wife is with him, include her. It is not necessary to invite her personally. If your wife accompanies you, she may or may not communicate with guest-wife beforehand. With wives along, dinner is *strictly social*.

BANQUETS

Observe *time limit* on cocktail hour, go to table promptly.

Stand briefly if introduced by chairman.

DON'T talk or *leave* during speeches.

Applaud speakers—congratulate them if possible.

Chapter 7

TABLE MANNERS

PLACE SETTINGS

BREAKFAST

1. Napkin
2. Bread and butter plate
3. Water glass
4. Cup and saucer
5. Butter knife*

6. Fruit
7. Coffee
   (Extra spoon provided
   if cereal is ordered.)

* Butter knife may be small, placed on bread and butter plate instead of on table with other flatware.

57

LUNCH & DINNER

Salad fork
Luncheon/dinner fork
Luncheon/dinner knife
Soup spoon
Butter knife
Spoons for coffee and dessert

Cup and saucer included in place setting at lunch, but at dinner are added when coffee is served. If fruit or seafood is ordered, spoon or cocktail fork is provided. If dessert requires fork, it is placed on table when dessert is served.

BANQUET

Place settings sketched
in the
Imperial Suite
atop the
Conrad Hilton Hotel
Chicago

Banquet place setting is same as dinner with wine and champagne glasses, dessert spoon and fork, and finger bowl added. Spoon (or cocktail fork) far right is for first course.

Dessert plate, with dessert fork and spoon, doily and finger bowl, precede serving of dessert. Place fork and spoon on table beside plate, left and right, finger bowl and doily above fork, left. Use fork *or* spoon, or both. After dessert, dip fingertips in finger bowl, dry on napkin.

wrong

Keep your "face out of plate." *Don't* lean over plate with each bite (mouth to food).

Don't sit sideways at table.

Don't hold napkin by corner and shake out, tuck in, or clutch constantly in left hand and wave in air as you talk. Don't be "dainty"—but your napkin is *not* a mop.

right

Food is brought to mouth. Lean forward slightly as you eat, knees under table, napkin on knees. (If large, napkin is handier only partially unfolded.)

Wipe your mouth without mopping, using one or both hands.

wrong

KNIFE and FORK—CUTTING

Wrong grip on fork. Forefinger *too far down* on knife blade.

Never hold luncheon or dinner knife like this. *Wrong* grip on fork, elbows pointed out.

right

KNIFE and FORK—CUTTING

This is the *only right way* to hold knife and fork when cutting: right forefinger on knife *just above* or at *joining* of handle and blade, left forefinger on fork *above* joining of handle and tines. Fork tines are curved *toward* you. Elbows down.

wrong

CUTTING and EATING

Don't hold fork like this or cut meat all at one time.
(Knife above is in proper position.)

right

CUTTING and EATING

Cut one piece of meat (no more than two) at one
time, eat it with left hand as shown, *twisting* wrist *toward*
mouth, holding knife as shown, *elbow in*. It is unnecessary
(but not improper) to lay knife on plate and shift fork to
right hand with each bite. (Compare with illustration on
next page for eating with fork alone.)

wrong

EATING WITH FORK ALONE

Never hold fork like this or let knife (or fork) hang off edge of plate.

Never place knife and fork like this nor put them so near edge they fall off when plate is removed.

Don't hold silver in your hand when passing plate.

right

EATING WITH FORK, KNIFE ON PLATE

Eat vegetables, salad, etc., with fork in right hand, *knife on plate*, cutting edge *toward* you.

Position of knife and fork when finished: tines up *or* down, cutting edge *toward* you.

wrong

COFFEE and TEA

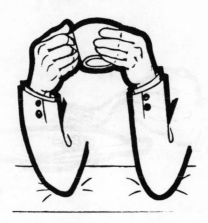

Don't drink (or eat) with elbow or elbows on table, both hands on cup. *Never* extend little finger.

Never leave spoon in cup.

right

COFFEE and TEA

Hold cup like this, fingers curved in, spoon always on saucer after sugar and cream added.

wrong

Don't pass cup alone for refill.

Never hand cup (without saucer) or pitcher to anyone with your hand covering handle.

right

Pass *both* cup and saucer for refill.

Pitcher, mug, paper cup or cup with disposable paper
liner (no saucer) are passed with handle pointing *toward*
person receiving it.

71

wrong

GLASSWARE

Don't drink with food in mouth or get food on rim of glass.

Don't hold glass with fingers at top—especially someone else's glass!

right

GLASSWARE

Hold glass like this.

wrong

SOUP

Don't spoon *toward* you when eating soup or tip bowl toward you.

Don't eat soup from tip of spoon, scrape spoon on edge of bowl or leave spoon in cup or bowl.

right

SOUP

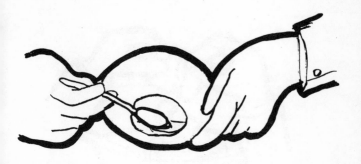

Spoon out when eating soup. Bowl or cup may be tipped (away from you).

Soup is eaten from *side* of spoon, may be drunk from *cup*.

wrong

Don't break crackers in soup all at one time.

SANDWICHES

Don't eat sandwich whole.

76

right

Spoon *always* on saucer or plate when not being used.

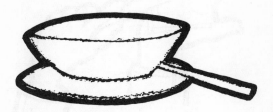

SANDWICHES

Cut sandwich in half with knife, eat with fingers.

wrong

BREAD and ROLLS

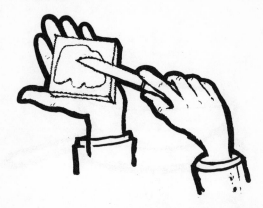

Never lay bread on palm of hand or on table and butter all at one time. *Don't* cut rolls or bread in half with knife.*

Never push food with fingers or mop plate clean with bread or fork.

* Exception: Corn bread, crumbly muffins, etc., may be cut in half with knife (butter knife or spreader, if you have one) and hot rolls buttered while hot.

right

Slice of bread is *torn* in half or in quarters, one piece at a time, *buttered as eaten.* Hot breads are torn in half, buttered, broken in pieces as eaten. (See *exception,* preceding page)

Small piece of bread may be used as *pusher* or dropped in sauce or gravy, then eaten with fork.

wrong

OYSTERS AND CLAMS ON HALFSHELL
Don't pour sauce over oysters and clams and don't attempt to cut large ones with fork before eating.

SHRIMP COCKTAIL
Don't cut (or try to!) large shrimp with fork, either in dish or on plate.

CASSEROLES, PLATTERS, LARGE SALAD BOWLS
Don't eat directly from platter, casserole or bowl.

right

OYSTERS AND CLAMS ON HALFSHELL

Hold shell with left hand, with right hand detach from shell by twisting fork, dip in sauce, eat *whole*.

SHRIMP COCKTAIL

Shrimp are eaten from fork, either whole or in bites.

CASSEROLES, PLATTERS, LARGE SALAD BOWLS

Serve self with serving spoon alone or with fork in left hand holding food on spoon.

wrong

TABLE MANNERS—MISCELLANEOUS

Don't stuff mouth full with each bite, talk with mouth full, chew with mouth open, emphasize conversation by waving knife or fork.

Don't start to eat until others are served, unless at large table.

Never wipe silver with napkin before using, and don't use own fork or spoon to serve self from dish being passed, sugar bowl, etc.

right

TABLE MANNERS—MISCELLANEOUS

Chew with mouth closed.

Swallow food *before* talking.

Wait for others to be served before starting to eat, except at large table.

If silver is not clean, ask waiter to replace it.

Use serving pieces when serving self from platter, sugar bowl, etc.

wrong

Don't stir or mix food on plate or eat large pieces of lettuce or long spaghetti without cutting with knife or fork.

Don't smack, click teeth on silver, sip audibly, blow on food, chew ice, cough or sneeze without covering mouth, or blow nose noisily.

Never pick your teeth or chew a toothpick, rub your tongue vigorously over teeth, switch water around, etc.

Don't put ashes, matches, etc., on plate, or put cigaret out by dipping in water or coffee.

Don't bite food from fork or throw it into your mouth.

right

Eat food as it is served on plate without *mixing* or *stirring*. Crisp, dry bacon may be eaten with fingers.

Cut salad with knife, if necessary.

Eat quietly, without smacking, clicking teeth on silver, sipping audibly.

Cover your mouth when coughng or sneezing, and if you cannot avoid it, blow nose quietly.

Clean your teeth in strict privacy.

If you smoke, use ash tray. In private home, if ash trays are not provided, *don't* smoke unless you're sure it's acceptable.

Take food from fork or spoon *with lips.*

Remove bones, pits, etc., from mouth with thumb and forefinger (lips pressed together), slide through lips, place on edge of plate.

Lemon: To squeeze juice over fish, etc., hold lemon section between thumb and first and second fingers with rind under palm to avoid squirting.

wrong

Don't rise from chair to reach for anything, or reach and spear bread or rolls with fork.

Don't remove bones or pits with mouth open, or spit them out on plate or in napkin.

Don't use dinner knife to serve self square of butter or to add butter to vegetables.

right

Reach for anything within *easy* arm's length.

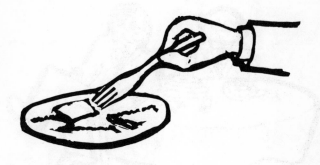

Use *fork* for serving self square of butter or adding butter to vegetables.

wrong

Don't leave table before others without excusing yourself.

Never stack dishes and push plate away when finished, turn and sit sideways, push away from table scraping chair noisily on floor.

Don't fold napkin or toss in plate when finished.

right

Say "excuse me" if you leave the table before others (for telephone call, etc.).

Stand if a woman stops at table. If all at table are men and another man stops, you do not rise unless introduced.

Place napkin, neatly *unfolded*, at the left of plate when finished.

Chapter 8

TIPPING

TIPPING

Every tip (in theory, anyway) is an individual trans-
action. Customs vary from city to city and there are
exceptions to everything.

You do not tip employees if No Tipping signs are dis-
played, employees of private clubs, or uniformed airline
employees.* Some country clubs permit tipping under
certain conditions.

In large dining rooms, you do not tip the headwaiter
(and *never* in coin) unless he preforms a special service,
such as reserving a choice table; nor do you tip the cap-
tain who may seat you and/or take your order, nor the
bus boy. *Tip the waiter who serves you.*

Fifteen percent has become standard in city restaurants,
with 20 percent expected in top bracket dining rooms
and night clubs. A common practice is to shade a 15 percent tip toward 10 percent or a 20 percent toward 15 on
the *amount in excess* of $12 or $15.

Over-tipping, especially on an expense account, is as
bad as under-tipping, but a generous tip in a restaurant
you patronize regularly is a good investment in service.

* Optional: Airport limousine drivers and porters who do no
more than hand you your luggage at baggage claim.

A group of men on a coffee break usually tip five cents each.

Don't assemble a tip in pennies, nickles and dimes, but if after paying a waiter, he brings you change roughly the amount of the tip, leave it all in the tray or on the table. If you pay a cashier, ask for change, take it back to the table.

An easy way to tip a cab driver is to pay him in paper money, ask for a specific amount of change. Do the same with porters, if you have no change.

The chart following contains a list of those you normally tip and *suggested* minimums and averages.

	MINIMUM	AVERAGE
WAITER* Snacks (counter or table)	10¢ on checks up to 50¢	10 to 15¢
Meals	15 to 25¢	15 per cent
BARTENDER	10¢	10 to 15 per cent
CAB DRIVER	15¢	15 per cent
CHECKROOM ATTENDANT	15¢	25¢
MEN'S ROOM ATTENDANT	15¢	15 to 25¢
BELLHOP	25¢	25 to 50¢ (more if he carries several bags)
DOORMAN Opening cab door (in or out) putting bag on sidewalk	NO TIP	
Carrying bag to desk	25¢	25¢

Hailing cab	25¢	25¢ (50¢ in bad weather)
Parking car	50¢	50¢
SKYCAP	25¢	25 to 50¢ (more if he waits, or for several bags)
REDCAP	25¢ per bag	25 to 35¢ per bag (Tip in addition expected)
PULLMAN PORTER	50¢	50¢ to $1.00 per night (more for extra service, drawing room, etc.)
BARBERSHOP		
Barber	25¢	25 to 50¢
Shoeshine/Porter	10¢	10 to 15¢

* *HEADWAITER*—For special service, not less than $1.00 folding money.

Chapter 9

GROOMING

wrong

Don't neglect daily shower, shave, use of deodorant, toothbrush, dental floss, mouthwash, nail brush.

Never have dirt under your nails, but DON'T *clean them in public!*

Don't neglect regular haircuts, wear sideburns, duck-tails, etc.

Never comb your hair in public.

right

**THESE ARE THE MINIMUM ESSENTIALS
OF GOOD GROOMING:**

A *daily* shower and shave.

The *daily* use of:
    Deodorant
    Toothbrush *and* dental floss, mouthwash
    Nail brush and nail file (for cleaning and shaping *in private*)
    Comb and brush (even crew cuts need brushing!)
    Clothes brush
    Shoe buffer

Unsightly moles, warts and wens on face and hands should be removed.

wrong

COATS

Don't fail to observe established company custom as to wearing coat during office hours.

Don't wear wrinkled suit, soiled pocket handkerchief, pocket flaps tucked in.

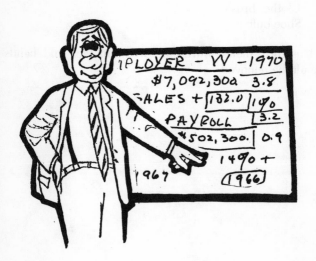

right

COATS

Company policy, the location of your desk, your contacts with the public, etc., determine when you wear your coat during business hours.

In general, wearing coat in your own office is optional. If you work for a large organization and see executives infrequently, put on your coat to go to their offices. If offices include more than one floor, company may prefer employees to wear coats going from floor to floor. Wear coat to greet a caller (not a co-worker) in your own office or in reception room, to go to lobby of building, at official meetings and conferences.

Some companies frown on short-sleeved shirts without coats. *Be alert to these company customs.*

wrong

Never wear your coat without *one button buttoned*—
at least when you're standing!

TIES

Don't wear ties too short or too long (below top of
trousers), and *don't* tie in a small hard knot.

right

Always wear your coat, center button buttoned:
At meals.

Social events—unless specified informal such as picnics, barbecues, etc. Take it along anyway; you can always remove it!

On the street, public conveyances, trains, planes.

When giving speeches, being photographed, appearing on TV, etc.

Shirt cuffs should show about one-half inch with arms down. Sports shirts (no tie) are not acceptable in business: city clubs and many restaurants will not admit you without tie and coat.

TIES

Knot should be easy, tie a little above trousers.

NEVER longer than just touching belt. Proportioned lengths are available: 52, 54, 56 inches. Select yours accordingly if you are above or below average height.

"Black tie" on an invitation means wear dinner jacket (tuxedo).

103

wrong

Don't let trousers sag, drape over instep, cover back of shoes.

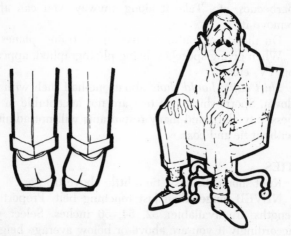

Don't wear scuffed shoes, run-over heels.
Never let socks wrinkle, sag, show bare leg.

right

Trousers should "brush leather"—just touch shoe tops or a little above.

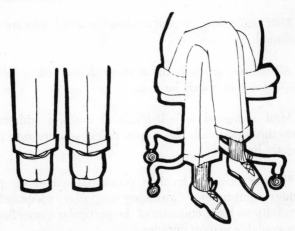

Shoes should be polished, *heels squared*.
SOCKS UP!

MISCELLANEOUS

It is still good manners to say "Good morning, *sir*" to the boss, to hold a door for a woman (but not several), to let women leave elevators first, unless you are directly in front.

Stand when a woman caller enters your office, but not for a co-worker unless she is a business superior who calls on you infrequently.

If introduced to a woman and she offers to shake hands, never say "Pardon my glove" or struggle to take it off—just shake hands and ignore the glove.

Refer to your wife as "my wife" to strangers, as "Marian" to your friends. She is *never* "the wife."

Another person's desk is private property. *Don't* open drawers without asking permission and *don't* be a desk "scanner" (try to read or see what is on another's desk).

Don't eavesdrop on conversations in which you are not included.

All salaries are personal matters. *Never* ask a fellow employee how much he makes.

Mail addressed to individuals at business address is sometimes personal. *Don't* open unless you are *sure* it is strictly business.

If your business involves occasional games of golf, bridge, tennis, etc. (assuming you play adequately), brush up on basic etiquette of the particular game. Books are available in most libraries.

The way you speak is important. Watch things like—

WRONG	RIGHT
Huh?	Sir?
Yeah	Yes or yes, sir
Gimme	Give me
I got	I have
Hafta or gotta	Have to
Goin', doin', etc.	Going, doing

QUALITY PAPERBACK BOOKS
Designed to Instruct and Entertain
Each book written by an expert in his field

Acting and Stage Movement, 95¢
Aeromodeling, $1.45
Amateur Psychologist's Dictionary, 95¢
Antique Furniture for the Smaller Home, 95¢
Archery, 95¢
Art of Riding, 95¢
Astrology, 95¢
Boy or Girl? Names for Every Child, 95¢
Cheiro's Book of Numbers, 95¢
Cheiro's Palmistry for All, 95¢
Cheiro's When Were You Born?, 95¢
Complete Guide to Palmistry, 95¢
Drama, 95¢
Find Your Job and Land It, 95¢
Fitness After Forty, $1.45
Gift Wrapping, 95¢
Golf at a Glance, 95¢
Guide to Personality Through Handwriting, $1.45
Health Foods and Herbs, 95¢
Heart Disease and High Blood Pressure, 95¢
Home Brewing Without Failures, 95¢
How to Be Healthy With Yoga, 95¢
How to Beat Personality Tests, $1.45
How to Train for Track and Field, 95¢
How to Win at Gin Rummy, 95¢
Instant Etiquette for Businessmen, 95¢
Judo and Self Defense, 95¢
Knots and Splices, 95¢

Laughter in a Damp Climate, $1.45
Lawn Tennis, 95¢
Magic of Numbers, 95¢
Manual of Sex and Marriage, $1.45
Mas Oyama's Karate, 95¢
Muscle Building for Beginners, 95¢
Mushroom Recipes, $1.45
131 Magic Tricks for Amateurs, 95¢
Painting and Drawing, 95¢
Practical Guide to Antique Collecting, 95¢
Production & Staging of Plays, 95¢
Profitable Poker, $1.45
Public Speaking, $1.45
Radio Astronomy and Building Your Own Telescope, 95¢
Remembering Made Easy, 95¢
Sailing Step by Step, 95¢
Shakespeare in the Red, 95¢
She Looks at Sex, 95¢
Slipped Discs, 95¢
Stamp Collecting for Fun and Profit, $1.45
Stomach Ulcers, 95¢
Student's Guide, $1.45
Successful Winemaking at Home, 95¢
3 Great Classics, $1.45
Upholstery, 95¢
Wake Up and Write, 95¢
Weightlifting & Weight Training, 95¢
Whole Truth About Allergy, 95¢
Woodturning, 95¢
You and Your Dog, 95¢
You Can Find a Fortune, $1.45
Your Allergic Child, $1.45